Frank Bridge
Three Pieces
for Organ

Andante moderato · Adagio · Allegro con spirito

NOVELLO PUBLISHING LIMITED

8/9 Frith Street, London W1V 5TZ

Order No: NOV 160068

Frank Bridge
1879-1941

Publisher's Note

Frank Bridge studied composition under Stanford, but it was his facility as a string player in chamber music (firstly violin, later viola) that occupied much of his earlier life. There were also many conducting engagements, from opera at the Savoy Theatre to the Proms.

His creative output was dominated by chamber music, the originality of which has been championed by many distinguished musicians, notably his pupil Benjamin Britten. Bridge also wrote a good deal of keyboard music, principally for piano, with a few pieces for organ.

This set of three was first published in 1905. It includes the *Adagio in E*, a piece popular with organists ever since.

NOVELLO & COMPANY LIMITED

Photograph of Frank Bridge reproduced by permission of Radio Times Hulton Picture Library.

Swell *pp* (Celestes.)
Choir *p* (Gamba, Gedackt & Dulciana.)
Great *p* (Wald Flute 8 f!)
Pedal soft 16 & 8 f!
Swell to Great
Swell to Choir
Swell to Pedal

ANDANTE MODERATO in C minor

Frank Bridge

ADAGIO in E major

Swell *pp* (Celestes.)
Choir *p* (Lieblich Gedackt.)
Great soft Diaps.
Pedal soft 16 & 8 ft.
Swell to Great
Swell to Choir
Swell to Pedal

Frank Bridge

12097

ALLEGRO CON SPIRITO in B♭ major

Frank Bridge

Swell Full
Great Full
Choir Full
Pedal Full
Swell to Great
Swell to Choir
Swell to Pedal
Great to Pedal

Gt

Sw.

(Gt to Ped.)

f

12098